DREAM JOBS IN STADIUM AND SPORTS FACILITY OPERATIONS

KATHY FURGANG and ADAM FURGANG

ROSEN
PUBLISHING®

New York

Published in 2015 by The Rosen Publishing Group, Inc.
29 East 21st Street, New York, NY 10010

First Edition

Library of Congress Cataloging-in-Publication Data

Furgang, Kathy.
Dream jobs in stadium and sports facility operations/by Kathy
and Adam Furgang.
p. cm.—(Great careers in the sports industry)
Includes bibliographical references and index.
ISBN 978-1-4777-7529-5 (library binding)
1. Sports—Vocational guidance—Juvenile literature. 3. Sports
facilities—United States—Juvenile literature. 4. Sports facilities—
United States—Management. I. Furgang, Kathy. II. Title.
GV415.F87 2015
796—d23

Manufactured in the United States of America

CONTENTS

Sports stadiums can have their moments of unexpected excitement. Here, a Washington Nationals fan is taken into custody by Los Angeles Dodgers' stadium security for running onto the field during a game.

The most exciting moments in sports come when teams make it all the way to the championship game, go through that last exciting play-off game, and then finally win the title for the season. Crowds go wild in the stadium stands, and millions of people watching the game on television erupt with excitement—or disappointment, depending on the team they are rooting for.

In any World Series baseball play-off game, you might see scores of players and coaches rush onto the playing field to celebrate the victory. The same might happen at the end of a Super Bowl game or at the end of professional basketball championship games. The players want to celebrate their victory in the playing arena.

But behind the scenes, you will see a different reality. There are hundreds of staff working off the court, behind the dugout, and in the locker rooms to keep sports facilities running smoothly. The work that these people do may go completely unrecognized, with spectators noticing only when these professionals *don't* do their job. The work of people in the field of stadium and sports facility operations is crucial for fans to enjoy watching the games, players to safely play the games, and even the media to properly get access to where they need to be to report about the games. A sports stadium works like a very complex machine, with all parts interacting in combination with each other to ensure that the public stays safe and can experience the event in an enjoyable way. Operators of sports facilities have the ultimate goal of public safety in mind, but they also hope to have spectators leave with a positive experience, looking forward to returning to the facility again in the future.

The work available at sports stadiums and sports facilities is vast. When fans rush onto the field at the end of a championship game, there are security staff who make sure everyone stays safe. And what good would those security workers be if the stadium's communication systems were not up and running properly so that messages could be sent around the giant facility in a matter of seconds? Coordination among departments within the facility is needed to ensure that the event as a whole is successful for the public.

There are dangers to holding public events without proper management in the areas of security, crowd control, sanitation, food service, and first aid and medical response. Each stadium has custodial staff who make sure the stadium is clean when people leave, spending hours prepping every spot in the stadium for the next event. They communicate with management offices to inform them of issues, to request backup help, and to keep them informed of any other pertinent issues relating to their job. When all goes well, the stadium runs like a well-oiled machine; fans can pay attention to the game and have a good time. And a good experience for the fans is the ultimate goal of people with a career in stadium and sports facility operations. There are a wide variety of careers available within this field, and many provide room for growth and promotion to managerial positions.

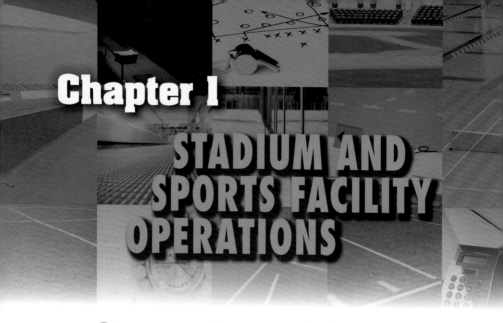

Chapter 1

STADIUM AND SPORTS FACILITY OPERATIONS

Some sports stadiums can employ hundreds of people. In the United States alone, there are over two hundred sports stadiums. Add to that the scores more that are in Canada, and you have endless opportunities for beginning a career in the stadium operations field. In Canada, the Olympic Stadium in Montreal seats nearly 60,000 people. The stadium was the site of the 1976 Summer Olympics, but it is now the home to both the Montreal Impact pro Canadian soccer team and the Montreal Alouettes, a Canadian pro football team. The coordination needed to manage a stadium that houses two pro teams makes the job even more challenging.

In the United States, the largest stadium is Michigan Stadium, in Ann Arbor, Michigan, home to the University of Michigan Wolverines football team. The stadium has held that title since it opened in 1927 with 109,901 seats.

There is a difference between different sports venues. A stadium is generally considered a large outdoor facility with tiers of seats surrounding a large field or stage. Stadiums are usually used for professional soccer, football, and baseball games. Many music concerts are also held in stadiums so that very large crowds can be accommodated. An arena is usually considered an indoor structure used for indoor sports such as basketball or ice hockey. Both kinds of structures can hold thousands of spectators and bring in millions of dollars each year.

However, sports can be played in structures on an even smaller scale. The field of sports facility operations also includes batting cages, ice-skating rinks, indoor

Montreal's Olympic Stadium can accommodate as many as 58,000 fans during one event. The stadium must be equipped to handle such large crowds safely and efficiently.

running or biking tracks, swimming pool facilities, rock climbing wall facilities, and health clubs. Anywhere that people gather to practice or play sports can be considered a sports facility. The facilities require special equipment and people with special training. The people who maintain the property may also need special knowledge about how the facility is used.

Although facilities such as health clubs and batting cages are much smaller than professional stadiums, there are many more of them throughout every state and province, opening the job opportunities even wider for people interested in

Some college football stadiums hold as many fans as professional league sites. Michigan Stadium, home of the Michigan Wolverines, holds close to 110,000 people.

getting involved in the field. Smaller venues may require the same person to take on a wider range of responsibilities than people doing those same jobs in larger venues. For example, a small health club may have only a dozen employees, while a stadium may employ hundreds. The general jobs of security, maintenance, scheduling, and event planning must be done at both places. There may be far fewer people at the health club to get the work done, however. Even though the events are on a much smaller scale, the organizational skills needed to plan an event are the same no matter what the venue.

VENUES LARGE AND SMALL

The kind of venue someone works in may often be a matter of choice. Some people prefer working in smaller places, getting to know clients and having a more personal relationship with coworkers and the public. That kind of person would be much better suited to a relatively small facility, such as an ice-skating rink. The day-to-day events in a large stadium may be overwhelming for some people. At the same time, some people prefer to work in the large stadium environment because they want to be close to the professional level of a sport. They are excited by the thought of working with professional athletes or helping to plan widely publicized events covered by the media. They may like to specialize in one narrow end of the business so that they can get to know it very well.

Some people may not have the opportunity to choose which kind of venue they work in. But if given the chance, it would help to think about the kind of person you are and which kind of venue you would enjoy working in most. When people are satisfied with their jobs, they may end up having a happier life overall. They may spend less time thinking that their job doesn't suit them, that they wished they could work in a more intimate environment, or that they would prefer to work with the public. What kind of dream environment would you imagine in the area of stadium and sports facility operations? The kind of

The Astoria Play Center and Swimming Pool is one of the largest public recreational facilities in the United States. Located in Queens, New York, the facility has been open to the public since 1936.

environment you imagine for yourself may help direct you to find the job that suits you best.

A VARIETY OF JOBS

You don't have to be a die-hard football fan to have an exciting career working at a professional football stadium. At the same time, you don't need to be a pro baseball player or trained coach to manage a batting cage or maintain a local baseball field. The job that a behind-the-scenes facility operator does is different from the job that the athlete on the field does. A love of the game is often what attracts a person to facility operations, but you don't have to be in the game to make a facility run smoothly.

Facility operators often feel a sense of pride about the work they do when they see a filled stadium or a crowded facility and know that people are enjoying their leisure time there. No matter whether you are working, on a scale as large as Yankee Stadium in the Bronx, New York, or at your local health club, many jobs related to the work are similar.

For example, some people are in charge of the daily events of the office. Whenever a business employs more than a few people, there are many office details to attend to. Making sure computers, printers, telephones, and other equipment are running smoothly is an important job of the office manager as well as the people who work for the office manager. Interviewing and hiring people may come under this department if there is no human resources department in the facility. The larger a facility is, the more positions and smaller departments there will likely be to handle different responsibilities. People who work in office management must have great organizational and communication skills. They often work with other employees and must form good relationships with them to keep morale at the office high.

KEEP YOUR OPTIONS OPEN

While it is important to try to focus in on the type of job that might interest you in the sports facility operations field, it's also important to keep your options open and go where your experiences take you. For example, if you are learning about managing a health club, you may research and learn about the fields of sports therapy, personal training, or public health. People who specialize in these fields work in health clubs, so you would likely run across them in your own journey in exploring careers in health clubs. However, these jobs require different training from what the person who manages the club would have. If you feel that you have the skills and personality for a job in sports therapy or training, you may wish to pursue it. Keeping your options open to every possibility can help you land the job that satisfies you the most.

Another important division of facility operations is event management. In small facilities, employees may plan local charity events or agree to allow the public to use the facility for various events. Prices must be negotiated about the cost of each event, and dates and times must be agreed upon. After that, the planning of a given event can be very time consuming. A detail-oriented person would be good at a job in event management. Menus must be decided, and the source of the food must be obtained. If a sport facility does not have its own food services, the event manager must coordinate with outside caterers to arrange for food to be delivered at the right time. Interpersonal skills are important in event management, in addition to budgeting and organizational skills.

The security at a sports facility is particularly important for keeping a safe environment for the public to gather in. Larger facilities have large security staffs and may have a lot of training in security and possibly law enforcement. People in these departments are responsible for knowing safety requirements and escape plans for the public in the case of emergency. Communications is an important part of working in this department. The largest facilities have communications offices to send and receive messages quickly throughout the stadium. Smaller facilities will likely have fewer people working security and communications, simply because their facilities do not hold high-profile public events and far fewer people enter the facilities each day.

There are many jobs available in sports facilities. At New York's Yankee Stadium, one worker cleans the hallway floors while others perform maintenance on a computer kiosk.

Every facility, large or small, needs a good maintenance crew. Buildings that get a lot of public use need constant attention and maintenance to keep them in working order. That means much more than cleaning the bathrooms. Large outdoor stadiums use intense lighting to make a nighttime event look as bright as possible. The new Yankee Stadium, opened in 2009, uses twenty thousand lightbulbs throughout the stadium as well as 946 miles (1,522 kilometers) of electrical wire. Keeping a large place like this working requires constant attention by a large maintenance staff. Groundskeeping is often included in the area of maintenance. The playing fields must be immaculately groomed, and parking lots must be cleaned and maintained for public safety. The maintenance at smaller, local fields may include only groundskeeping on fields and in parking lots. The size of the facility dictates what kind of maintenance crew is needed.

Another important area of sports facility operations is sales. The number of tickets sold each season at a large facility runs into the millions of dollars and makes all of the other areas of facility operations possible. There are a wide variety of packages available for people who wish to buy tickets in large blocks, individually, for the season, or just for a single game. Group sales are an important part of the sales department. These sales bring in large amounts of money for the stadium and for the teams and performers that play at the stadium.

Booking and media relations are also important parts of facility operations. Without the booking of events and their coverage by the media, large stadiums would not be able to make enough money to maintain their own operations. Booking extra events at a stadium is a way to make extra money for the stadium, and the events bring media attention to the facility. Booking charity events also brings public attention to smaller arenas.

There is a wide variety of jobs available at sports facilities, both big and small. Each department in the field may have a hierarchy of jobs available, from the assistant level

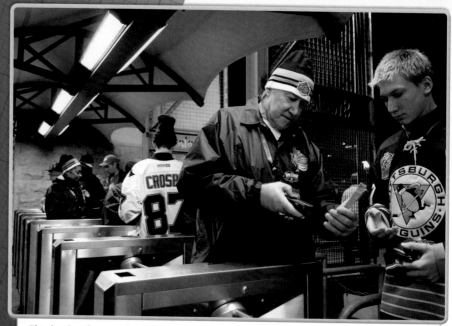

This hockey fan gets his ticket scanned by a facility employee as he enters a sports stadium to see the Pittsburgh Penguins play.

to the managerial level. There is such a wide variety of jobs available for people in sports facility operations that a person could explore different departments within the same company, keeping the same employer for years. This wide array can benefit an employee who is getting benefits from the company because he or she may be able to keep health insurance and build up a retirement account while still moving between departments and exploring different work opportunities.

Chapter 2
GETTING READY EARLY

Deciding on the right career can take a long time. Some people change their minds several times about what career path to choose. It's perfectly normal for people to change their minds and experiment with different career possibilities. The field of stadium and sports facility operations is one that allows a lot of exploration for people with a wide variety of education levels. The first and most important thing to do is to jump in and get involved early.

Many people fall into careers accidentally, never even thinking about looking into possible careers while they are still in school. It helps to make the leap and think of the benefits of early career exploration.

For the field of stadium and facility operations, it is useful to learn about as many sports as possible. You are probably interested in this type of career because you are already interested in sports. However, many people don't have a very wide knowledge of the kinds of sports and facilities that are out there. You may have gone to a professional football or baseball game and sat in the stands, in awe of the huge crowd and the magnificent stadium. You may have gone to a basketball game and become entranced by the magnificent echoing sound of the crowd's cheers bouncing off the walls and ceiling of the stadium. The sound of the athletes' sneakers screeching to a noisy stop against the shiny, polished court may have made you really appreciate how amazing the facility is and how lucky you are to witness a game there.

There are many other sports that don't get as much thought as the top three professional games of baseball, basketball, and football. Think about the different kinds of sports and physical activities that people play and engage in: soccer, ice-skating, gymnastics, ice hockey, yoga, Pilates, Zumba, aerobics, weight lifting, rock climbing, Ultimate Frisbee, lacrosse—the list goes on and on. Each of these sports and activities is practiced in a particular way, and people gather to play and practice them in specific kinds of venues. One sports club might have an indoor track, weight room, aerobics room, or Pilates or yoga studio, in addition to a swimming pool and cycling room. Observing what is around you in your community can help you understand how complex some facilities can be.

Ice-skating rinks are interesting to look at for their technical needs. Creating an indoor ice rink for figure skating or competitive hockey involves large equipment

There are many more smaller sports facilities throughout North America than there are sports stadiums. At this sports facility in Williamsburg, Virginia, students take a yoga class.

for making and cleaning the ice, as well as a good deal of background space for storing the equipment. Requesting a behind-the-scenes tour of one of these facilities with an adult can help give you a sense of what goes on and how one kind of facility differs from another.

OBSERVE CAREFULLY

When you are at a stadium enjoying a game, take notice of the people working around you. There are teams of workers for just about every task you can imagine. During rain delays at professional baseball games, you may see a team of workers spread a huge tarp over the field. Think about what those workers might normally do during a day and where they keep a giant tarp like the one they are unraveling over the field! The workings of a stadium are intricate and fascinating. Spend some time looking around when you are at a professional or semiprofessional game. However, only go where you are designated to go. Never go into private areas that are not open to the public. If you would like a tour of the facility, be sure to arrange it ahead of time by calling the stadium and asking questions. You may find that the people running the stadium are very helpful and

Sports facility workers may have unexpected duties. These workers cover Wrigley Field for a rain delay during a Chicago Cubs baseball game.

accommodating or you may find that they are not willing to open their stadium to the public. Be respectful of the people you speak to and the decisions they make. Remember that there is always more than one way to explore and learn about a topic.

LOOK IT UP

If you are interested in stadiums, you'll find some good information on the Internet or in your local library. Construction companies such as Turner Construction list details about their architectural projects, including some of the largest stadiums in the country. These sites can give you fascinating facts about the building details, such as the number of seats, square footage, building materials, and other information. The sites are meant to promote companies' architectural and construction experience, but the information is interesting to anyone who wants to find out more about some of the most complex structures in sporting. The sites show behind-the-scene pictures of control rooms for communication and security, dining areas, and other parts of the facilities. The pictures show open floor plans that accommodate many people, and they also list the special features of each stadium, such as players' lounges, therapy rooms, workout rooms, and team doctors' offices.

Looking for books in your local library is also a good way to learn more. Even if your library does not have information about sports facilities specifically, you can look for books that discuss other careers in sports, such as sports management, sports therapy, sports broadcasting, and other careers that require an understanding of the field of sports.

VOLUNTEERING AND INTERNING

One way to start exploring careers early is to become a volunteer or intern. Volunteers work with no pay, doing a variety of tasks for an employer. Interns often work for free as well, but in exchange for school credits. Internships are most common for college students, but some high schools team up with local businesses to offer internship experiences for students. Ask your guidance counselor about the internship opportunities that are available. Some schools may work with students to create a custom internship based on the students' needs and interests. Even if no school credit can be offered, your school may be willing to help you seek out a non-credit internship. Expressing your interests to your guidance counselor can help him or her find an employer that is right for you.

Whether you live in a big city near a major stadium or in a small town with only one or two health clubs, you should be able to find some kind of sports facility to inquire with. These facilities may use young volunteers or interns to help with office tasks such as

Intern Eric Glass gets a rare opportunity to defend Miami Heat guard Ray Allen during a pregame practice at the American Airlines Arena in Miami, Florida.

GET INVOLVED

Whether you intern, volunteer, or just play sports for fun, it always helps to get involved by going to a local sports facility. Get involved with a local sports organization or recreation club run by your town. These options may be cheaper than a club membership, and they may use local facilities for their events. There are also nonprofit organizations that hold community events. Get involved in a fund-raiser, charity walk, or other local event to see how it is run. Be a spectator at amateur or professional sporting events in your area. Or, better yet, participate in sporting events yourself to see the demands that athletes may put on a sports facility and how their demands are met by the staff. The more you get involved and learn on your own, the more you will be prepared to pursue a career in the field.

Volunteers may get involved in community and charity events, such as this breast cancer charity race in North Carolina, the Susan G. Komen Wilmington Race for the Cure.

filing or other administrative duties. Someone who is interested in the exciting world of stadiums and sports facilities may feel that filing and administrative duties are not particularly engaging. It may seem boring or not a good representation of the business as a whole. But think again. The paperwork that you would come in contact with will give you a good idea about what the industry is about and how it works. The tasks that you see other people doing will also give you a sense of the varied parts of the business.

An intern at a health club might come in contact with paperwork regarding memberships, promotions, new classes, or service calls for gym equipment, locker room facilities, or even vending machines. You may come in contact with information regarding customer complaints or suggestions, or upcoming charity fund-raisers. These experiences will teach you more about the field and give you an idea about what you might want to focus on or study in college or paying jobs you might wish to have after high school.

A volunteer might be put in a position to deal with the public directly. Working at the front desk of a health club, checking in customers, or answering phones are some of the duties that a volunteer might be asked to perform. Whether you are interning or volunteering, you will be put in contact with people who work in the field you are interested in. You will be surrounded by people who may have experience in budgeting, staffing, security, first aid, and possibly even crowd control or crisis management. That will give you a sense of how people work and what their day-to-day jobs are like. You can't be expected to learn everything about what other people do when you are an intern or volunteer, but you can get a sense of which jobs seem most interesting to you and what kinds of personal and professional skills are required for different jobs.

Gym employees with good interpersonal skills can answer clients' questions, help them sign up for classes, and make them feel at home at the facility.

ASKING QUESTIONS

You may be filled with questions about the kind of work each person at a stadium or sports facility does. What better way to get answers to those specific questions than to set up an informational interview with someone who works in the field. Many professionals are happy to share information with younger people who show an interest in their line of work. It helps to call a local facility to ask if anyone would be able to sit with you and discuss the industry. You may even wish to call a major stadium and conduct a telephone interview if you don't live near the stadium.

Sometimes public relations workers will be the ones to speak to the public. Always have a list of questions ready ahead of time in case someone wishes to preview your questions before granting the interview.

If you are indeed granted an interview, be as professional and polite as possible. You might wish to ask preplanned questions about the skills, education, and training needed to do the job. Questions about the day-to-day responsibilities and the chance for advancement would also be appropriate. It may not be appropriate to ask about salary, but questions about benefits could be asked because it does not involve personal information. Listen carefully to the answers and form follow-up

FIND A MENTOR

A mentor is a person who has experience in a certain area who can pass that knowledge and experience to a younger or less experienced person. A mentor can be a supervisor at an internship or volunteer position, a coach, or even a relative or other person you know who works in the business. A mentor might be available to explain industry news to you or to fill you in on new developments in the sports world. Many successful business people start their careers with a mentor to help orient them in the business.

questions for points you don't understand. You may wish to record the interview to reference again later, but make sure the person you are interviewing knows that he or she is being recorded. Another alternative is to take notes during the conversation or directly afterward.

If you are not granted an interview, continue to be polite and professional to the people you are in contact with. You may wish to ask again at a later time or to ask another facility if they are willing to offer an informational interview.

READ ALL ABOUT IT

Sports journals and sports news offer a lot of information about the business as a whole. It helps to be well informed about sports and to learn as much as you can about the business. If you intern or volunteer at a sports facility, you will find that many professionals keep up to date in their field by reading industry journals and keeping up on news in sports. That kind of knowledge is not limited to people in the field. Anyone can read industry journals. Local libraries carry many specialized sports publications, and some may also be available online.

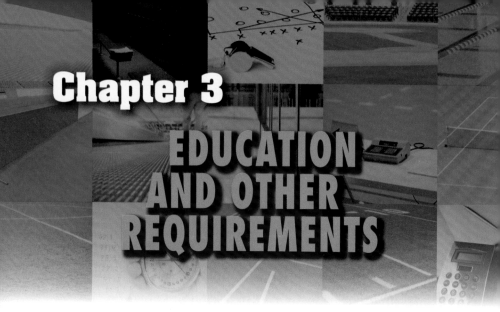

Chapter 3
EDUCATION AND OTHER REQUIREMENTS

If you have done a little research into the area of stadium and sports facility operations and decided that it still intrigues you, it's time to think about pursuing an education that can help you succeed in that field. The area of sports facility operations offers a very wide variety of jobs, and people involved in the field vary in their educational backgrounds. You may find many people in the field with no college degree at all, others with a two-year associate's degree, others with a four-year bachelor's degree, and still others with a graduate degree such as a master's degree. The level of education that different employees have depends on the work they are expected to do. For example, people working in the maintenance department may not have college degrees, but their supervisors or managers may be college educated. The same kind of hierarchy exists in nearly all of the departments. Some people working in the food services department may have no formal education past the high school level. However, managers or directors

Stadium employees have all levels of education and work their way through the ranks. This snack vendor at a Toronto Blue Jays game has an entry-level position.

of the department may have bachelor's or even master's level degrees in food services, hospitality, or food industry management. The level of responsibility increases as people are promoted to managerial and director positions. Some people continue their educations part-time while still working on the job and making money.

COLLEGE DEGREES IN SPORTS

There are plenty of college degrees associated with sports, both at the associate's level and the bachelor's level. An associate's degree typically takes two years of full-time

COLLEGE INTERVIEWS AND ESSAYS

If you are applying to colleges that offer degrees in sports management or sports marketing, express your interest in being part of these programs. Specifically state in your interview, college essay, or application that you would like to be involved in the program and hope to use the education you get at the school to start a career in sports. Communicate your interest in sports in your essay, if appropriate. Many students are unsure about what they wish to do when they get into college, so someone who shows direction and purpose will look good to potential schools.

classes, while a bachelor's degree takes four years of full-time classes. Sports management is one of the most common degrees to get. The courses give a good overview of the different jobs in the sports industry. Courses may also deal with new technologies in the sports industry, as well as how to manage businesses related to the sports field. This major can give you a great overview of the many fields that overlap in sports, such as marketing, economics, sociology, psychology, history, business, and even statistics.

Another degree that involves sports is sports marketing. In this major, students learn about how sports are

This student practices his swing at the University of Maryland Eastern Shore. The university offers the first golf management degree in the United States.

promoted and marketed to the public, including through advertisements, public relations, and interacting with the media. Larger sports stadiums may employ people with these specialties to help them promote and market their own stadium and sell more tickets to the public.

Sports law is another degree that would prove useful at large sports stadiums. Large contracts are negotiated between the stadium and teams, food vendors, broadcasters, and many other companies necessary for the smooth operation of a stadium. Someone who specializes in sports law knows a lot about contracting and legal negotiations with another party. Some large stadiums may have a legal department that takes care of all legal issues, including any lawsuits that might arise with guests, athletes, coaches, or employees. College courses would focus on understanding contracts, guidelines that regulate players and teams on and off the field, and important court cases that involved sports in the past. Those who major in sports law cannot practice law unless they also go to law school and get a professional law degree, called a Juris Doctor.

Other degrees related to sports are less likely to be used in taking care of sports facilities, such as sports journalism, coaching, sports science, kinesthesiology, fitness and nutrition, sports psychology, and sports journalism. Stadiums are likely to have people with all of these specialties working there in some way, but their jobs are not related to facility operations. For example, the coaches and fitness trainers who work with the athletes are part of the day-to-day operations of the stadium, but they do not work behind the scenes to make the actual stadium stay open, safe, and up and running. The same goes for the sports journalists and broadcasters seen at every game. While it is true that they are an important part of the stadium's operations, they do not work for the stadium. Their concentration is on the broadcasting of the game, and they are employed by the television station, newspaper, or cable network that their reports are meant for.

John McEnroe, Dick Enberg, and Mary Carillo work in the announcer's booth at the 2011 U.S. Open. Announcers usually work for the broadcaster, not the stadium.

Because you are interested in facility operations does not mean that you should not explore classes in these areas. The more you know about the sports business, the better. Learning about the wide variety of areas that touch the sports world can make you a better, more well-rounded employee.

COLLEGE DEGREES IN BUSINESS

Not all colleges have programs in sports management or sports marketing. It helps to look for these schools if you are interested in them, but it is not always possible to find what you are looking for or to be accepted into the schools that may have been your top choices. A standard business degree would also be very useful for someone who wants ultimately to work in sports facility operations. Business degrees and business programs are widely available from most colleges, universities, and community colleges, and they are also offered both on the associate's degree level and the bachelor's degree level.

There are a couple of kinds of business degrees that people can focus on, no matter what type of business they ultimately choose to work in. A business administration degree offers students a background in areas such as accounting, economics, finance, and technology and information systems. These are the skills that are needed to make a business run.

A business management degree focuses more on getting people into leadership roles in business, such as problem solving, thinking critically, thinking of entrepreneurial ideas, and resolving conflicts. There is an overlap between the coursework and study of the two degrees, but the major differences are that business management trains people for leadership, while business administration trains people in basic business skills. The terms are sometimes used interchangeably in some schools, and not all schools offer both degrees. Compare the courses offered by schools that offer each degree. You may find that many of the courses overlap so that students who focus on either degree are well rounded.

The business course options are almost endless when taking generalized coursework and then applying it later to the sports industry when looking for a job. Even people who do not wish to get an associate's degree or bachelor's degree in business can get a business certificate. This may include taking a few courses at a college, or even online, and the certificate can be a helpful tool in getting a job. The courses will likely focus on accounting, marketing, finance, principles of organization, and management skills.

After receiving a general degree or certificate in business, you will look more attractive to an employer in the area of sports facility operations. Your knowledge of business, finance, marketing, and accounting will help in the running of the sports facility.

Some people begin working in a field and then return to college part-time to continue their education while they are still working. This is a good way to let your employer know that you are interested in moving up in your industry and are not afraid to take on more responsibility. In some cases, employers will pay for some or all of the expenses of sending an employee back to school to get a degree. The employer may require that the employee stay with the company for a certain amount of time after the degree is earned, but it can also mean a raise and more money for the employee. These kinds of offers from employers usually come from larger, more established companies, such as large stadiums instead of smaller facilities or health clubs. This does not mean that larger companies value their employees more, it is simply because they have more money for professional development of their employees. When looking for a job, professional development is something to consider, in addition to the salary and other benefits that are offered.

OTHER SPECIALTY DEGREES

Not all jobs in the field of sports stadiums and facility operations require a business degree. Many other jobs require specialties in other areas, such as food services, communication technology, computer technology, engineering, or security. People with degrees in these fields can look for work in the sports industry in a stadium or other sports facility. Their knowledge and expertise will make them valuable to the employer, and their day-to-day job may not require knowledge of sports at all.

Check colleges for the variety of programs they offer, and then choose something that interests you and provides versatility. If you can't find work in a sports stadium

Security is an important specialty at stadiums. These fans meet with heightened security measures at Minute Maid Park in Houston, Texas, after the Boston Marathon bombing in 2013.

or other sports facility, you would still have many opportunities to look for work in other fields. As with people with business specialties, people with other specialized degrees have an opportunity to move up in their field as they continue to work for their employer.

WORKING IN THE FIELD

Not everyone goes to college after high school, or even takes part in a community college or pursues an online certificate. There are many opportunities to go to work right out of high school. The options are wide open in the field of sports facilities. Looking in the classified ads may be the best way to determine what a facility may need at any given time because their needs are so vast. They may need plenty of help in which a college degree is not needed at all. Custodial duties, working with food vendors serving and selling food, ripping tickets at the entry gates of the stadiums, and selling memorabilia are just a few examples of paying jobs that need to be filled in the industry. In terms of security, people may be needed to check bags at the gates, keep an eye out for suspicious activity, patrol parking lots or seating areas, or help put emergency plans into effect. These jobs may require on-the-job training, just as any job would require a certain amount of explanation and training. Similarly, some administrative duties would not require employees to have secondary degrees. It

Vendors are busy selling memorabilia to LA Kings hockey fans at Staples Center in Los Angeles, California.

always helps to have a high school degree when looking for permanent employment, but many jobs in a stadium don't require that workers have any formal education.

There may well be opportunities to advance for those who prove to be good employees. Someone who is professional, is courteous with the public, and comes to work promptly and regularly will likely get good performance reviews and regular raises. You may be promoted after a number of years and even be given more responsibilities. If you show your supervisors that you are responsible and can handle tasks with

MAKING THE INTERVIEW COUNT

When interviewing for a job at a stadium or other sports facility, always look professional and be courteous and polite. Show your interest in the company as a whole. Ask the interviewer what opportunities might be available for advancement down the road. Make sure to express a sincere interest in the job you are being considered for at the moment, but also convey that you are willing to stay at the company for a while, looking ahead to a fulfilling future with the company. An interview is the first glimpse the company gets of you, and it's the only way the company can make its decision about whether it would like to work with you. Make the interview count by showing your interest, enthusiasm, and potential.

little help, you may be able to apply for open managerial positions that arise in the future. That may mean becoming a supervisor yourself. Even if you don't have a formal college education, you may have the skills that are needed to do many of the jobs in the industry.

Chapter 4

JOBS IN SPORTS FACILITY OPERATIONS

When you think of a sports facility, you may not think of the wide variety of venues that are open to the public. Every fitness club, YMCA, community recreation center, golf club, sports program, public recreation area, and military sports complex falls under the category of a sports facility. Each one requires qualified people who can offer safe, quality sports access to the public. Workers require a wide range of knowledge about sports as it pertains to trained athletes, as well as young children and senior citizens. Sports facilities are often very busy places, and the people who make the business work smoothly from behind the scenes do a wide range of jobs. The jobs listed here are general categories of jobs. Smaller facilities may have one person combine two or more categories of responsibilities. Some facilities may use different titles to describe the same job. However, these are the general categories of jobs that need to be filled so that a sports facility can satisfactorily serve the public.

HUMAN RESOURCES MANAGER

The human resources manager is the person who is in charge of hiring all of the other people who work for the facility. Larger facilities may have an entire human resources department, but the job of the manager is to oversee the hiring needs of the company. A fitness club may need to hire coaches for amateur teams, tutors for after-school programs, lifeguards for the pool, personal trainers as part of membership services, or instructors for classes. The number of people who work for a sports facility may be in the hundreds. Some of the people

Managers get involved in all aspects of the facilities. Some specialize in different areas, such as hiring, finance, special events, or customer service.

may be part-time workers who teach only one or two classes per week. Others are supervisors or managers who work full-time.

A human resources manager must have excellent communication skills and be good at talking to people face to face to learn about their qualifications. The human resources manager may first talk to the manager who is looking for an employee to find out what qualifications the person should have who interviews for the job. The human resources department is the first step of the interview process. The manager goes through resumes and calls in people for an interview if they seem qualified. The manager then sends the most qualified people to be interviewed by the department head they would be working for. The human resources manager has a much broader understanding of the business and is not required to understand everything about the interviewee's qualifications. He or she explains any health or other benefits the company offers and weeds out unqualified candidates. A human resources manager may have several other people working in the department doing work at various levels.

EVENTS MANAGER

An events manager is in charge of planning and carrying through with special events at the facility. These may include walks or runs to benefit charities, concerts, corporate parties, or promotional events to advertise the facility. Event planning includes agreeing upon the right date and working through all the details, such as time, exact location, food that will be served, and any music that will be played. If the facility does not have its own food services, catering will have to be arranged, including the renting of tables to hold and serve the food.

Another responsibility of the events manager is agreeing upon a price that will be paid by the people arranging the event. This includes any proceeds that will go to charity and any that will go to the facility for payment.

Event managers often work with a team of people, including assistants. The people involved in organizing events should be outgoing and friendly because they work directly with the public. They may need a certain amount of physical strength if they will be setting up tables and chairs or carrying trays of food.

ATHLETICS DIRECTOR

The athletics director is in charge of all of the people who work at the facility in any sports-related capacity. This includes all of the teachers, coaches, instructors, lifeguards, and trainers who are in contact with the public. An athletics director may have a degree in sports or public health. He or she is expected to know about a wide variety of sports and how they differ in the way the human body is expected to perform for each. Public safety is the number one concern of the athletics director. The director makes sure that the teachers and coaches are well qualified and work well with the public, and that they are concerned with the safety of the club or facility members.

The injuries of club members are a great concern to the sports facility. The athletics director trains employees

WHAT'S IN A JOB TITLE?

If you go to a local sports facility or look up the titles of people who work there, you may find that the job titles do not match the titles mentioned in this section. You may see that the words "manager," "supervisor," and "director" are used interchangeably and that some people may be described as an executive director instead of just a director. The reason for this is that each facility makes its own job titles. The titles may depend on the size of the facility, the amount of time the person has worked there, the number of people the person oversees, and the education level of the person. For example, a supervisor may be promoted to manager, and a manager may be promoted to the level of director. A new supervisor may be hired because he or she has a master's degree in sports management or sports marketing. That person may be given the title of manager or director because of his or her formal education. The department that the person works in is the true indication of the kind of work he or she does.

so that they take public safety seriously and ensure that club members enjoy their experience.

BUILDING SUPERVISOR

The building supervisor is in charge of coordinating the work of the custodians, building contractors, pool services, and any other maintenance needed for the building. This responsibility may in some cases extend to lawn and parking lot care. It may also include overseeing the maintenance and servicing of gym equipment. The job of the custodial staff is very important when maintaining a clean, presentable, and safe building for the practice of sports. Broken or poorly maintained equipment or an unclean environment can invite injury to the people using the facility, which can in turn lead to lawsuits.

A building supervisor should be good in dealing with staff and have an excellent understanding of mechanics and cleaning services. Formal education may include training as an electrician, as a plumber, or in custodial services.

DIGITAL COMMUNICATIONS AND MEDIA SPECIALIST

Like all modern facilities, newer sports facilities make use of technology and digital communications. The communications and media specialist oversees how these technologies are used throughout the facility. The work may include understanding a complex intercom or walkie-talkie system that may be tied to a video monitoring system. These systems may be used for employee communication in a large facility, or they may be used as a security or safety feature to monitor members. Many facilities offer education classes, so the media specialists would be in charge of setting up or maintaining any equipment that falls under the category of communications technology, such as DVD

Communications specialists have an important job in making stadiums safe and keeping operations running smoothly.

presentations, PowerPoint demonstrations, or television hookups to provide live feeds for the media or for recording for later use.

Digital communications and media specialists must have a strong understanding of technology and how it works. They must keep up to date with current changes and updates to technology and be able to provide budget guidelines regarding when technologies should be replaced with new ones.

COMPUTER AND TECHNOLOGY SPECIALIST

Most modern facility offices have computer and technology specialists. The person in this position would be concerned with the computers on each employee's desk and the software used by the facility. This person could oversee a staff of technology specialists if the facility is very large, but these departments may be very small. The computer and technology specialist must have a strong ability to troubleshoot and solve problems. In addition, communications is integral to jobs in this area, so the person should have patience and good interpersonal skills. The computer department is often faced with difficult problems when a person's computer does not work, and the proper tone and attitude is needed to fix these problems.

The Olympic Training Center in Colorado Springs, Colorado, has large screen televisions and video delay systems. The technology helps provide athletes with quick feedback about their training.

ENROLLMENT SUPERVISOR

Sports facilities stay in business if they have good enrollment. The job of the enrollment, or membership, supervisor is to make sure that many people are joining and staying enrolled in the facility. This may mean working out payment plans with individuals or families. It often means coming up with promotions to attract new members or to make sure that current members renew their membership. The enrollment supervisor also works out price increases and determines the differences between individual, family, child, senior, and group membership prices.

The enrollment supervisor should have good interpersonal skills and be able to communicate well with the

YMCA employees can have a positive impact on the community and foster a love for sports and fitness.

public. Good math skills are expected, as well as the ability to work with money and credit cards.

EDUCATION PROGRAM COORDINATOR

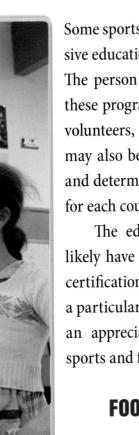

Some sports facilities, such as YMCAs, offer extensive education programs and child care programs. The person who is in charge of and coordinates these programs is responsible for hiring teachers, volunteers, and child care providers. The person may also be responsible for planning the courses and determining the age range that is appropriate for each course.

The education program coordinator would likely have a background in education, such as a certification as a teacher. This person may not have a particular background in sports but should have an appreciation and general understanding of sports and fitness.

FOOD SERVICES DIRECTOR

In the area of food services, some sports facilities offer not much more than a vending machine. Others might have an entire café or cafeteria open to the public. The director of this department is in charge of everything that occurs in the facility having to do with food, including how and when it is served. The director would be responsible for hiring a qualified staff of cooks and cleaning crews, and servers if necessary. The person may have a background in catering or restaurant services. During busy times, a food services department must be able to work under pressure, and the director should be able to pitch in and contribute to help ease any backup in the kitchen or in the line of customers.

The food services director must know a good deal about food safety laws and be able to set up a work environment that would pass inspection by the board of health. The director should be able to work well with and supervise others.

CUSTOMER SERVICE MANAGER

A sports facility that deals with the public will likely have a department that handles customer complaints and requests. The customer services manager oversees the way the facility deals with these communications. The manager or other staff members may take phone calls or meet in person with people who have complaints or questions. If necessary, the manager is often authorized to offer the customer compensation for his or her trouble. This may be in the form of a refund of membership fees, extra guest passes, or other perks such as meals at the café or cafeteria.

To follow through with a customer complaint, the manager would make sure that the problem the customer had is dealt with in a serious matter. For example, if the complaint was about a slippery surface in the pool area that caused an injury or a messy locker room or restroom, the customer service manager would then communicate with the building supervisor or custodial staff to make sure the problem is dealt with. People working in customer service must have good interpersonal skills, be professional and polite, and be able to problem solve under pressure.

ACCOUNTING AND FINANCE DIRECTORS

The person in charge of the money matters of a sports facility has an important job. The accounting and finances keep the facility open and operational. The director of this department may be responsible for setting a budget for the facility operations, including the salaries of any workers. The job would also entail determining how much incoming money is needed in terms of memberships and fund-raising to keep the facility from going over its scheduled budget.

An accounting and finance director should have a degree or other equivalent experience in math or finance. The person should also be able to communicate well with other department supervisors to determine their financial needs. The director may be in charge of several people in the department, or the department may be comprised of just one or two people.

EXECUTIVE DIRECTOR

Considering all of the different jobs that are needed to make a sports facility run efficiently, it makes sense that all of these departments should be overseen by a director or manager who can coordinate the activities between and among departments. The boss, or person in charge of everything, is often known as the executive director. In a small facility, this may also be the owner. This person is ultimately responsible for anything that goes wrong in the other departments or sections of the facility. This person should have a broad knowledge of sports, finance, building operations, and customer service. In larger facilities, this job may be filled by a person who has worked in other departments and understands the workings of the facility very well. This person should have very good communication and interpersonal skills.

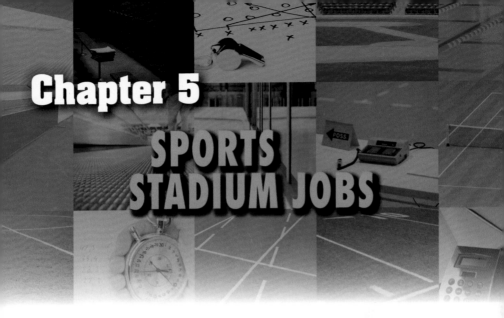

Chapter 5

SPORTS STADIUM JOBS

There are many differences between a sports stadium and a sports facility. The main difference is their function. A sports facility is usually intended for the public to use to perform or practice sports. A sports stadium is intended for the public to sit in stands as spectators of a professional sporting event or other large performance or show.

The main physical feature of a sports stadium is its seating. Most stadiums have more than ten thousand seats. That means that large numbers of people are flowing through the stadium at any given time. That also means that huge communication systems are needed so that all of those people can see and hear the event with no problems. Considering that each ticket probably costs at least $20, and often much more, the experience at the stadium should be enjoyable and worth the expense for the spectator.

To accomplish all of that for the stadium-going experience, there must be many people in place behind the

It takes many people behind the scenes to run a sports stadium, such as the BBVA Compass Stadium, which houses the Major League Soccer club the Houston Dynamos.

scenes to make the overall experience a positive one. Here are some of the most important jobs in sports stadium operations.

OFFICE MANAGER

An office manager is someone who might work in any kind of business maintaining office systems and supervising staff. The person might be responsible for

how and when employees are paid, buying office equipment, and making sure that the office equipment is in working order. These jobs pertain to the behind-the-scenes work and keeping office equipment working, such as computers, printers, and employee lounge equipment. It does not refer to working with the equipment in the stadium for use during public events, such as vending machines, vendor cash registers, ticket machines, and other devices. The back workings of a stadium are as much of a business as in other office buildings, with people working behind desks, doing accounting business, interviewing new employees, and filing paperwork. The everyday activities of many businesses are similar and require similar skills from their employees. People with good organizational skills and who have a professional manner can excel in the area of office management. Working well with other people is also a requirement because office managers frequently interact with other employees. Sometimes they settle disputes, while other times they organize office events or field complaints about problems in the office.

For a sports fan, a sports facility would be a fun place to come to work every day, even if you worked in a back office. Some of the daily work will involve sports on some level, whether it is scheduling events, answering phone calls from athletes or coaches, or ordering equipment or materials that will be used during games. The nature of the work is extremely varied in the area of office management.

Some sections of a sports stadium may seem like any other office building. There are mailrooms with an interoffice mail department for delivery and pickup. There are likely several conference rooms for meetings with staff and clients. There are computer hookups with a technology department to keep all computers up and running for business. The back offices also include a human resources section to help hire or fire employees, then replace them when needed.

The business offices will also coordinate any kind of plans for construction or renovation of the stadium. This will mean meeting with architects to discuss the stadium's needs, reviewing plans, and overseeing contracts and work schedules in the stadium.

The business offices will likely also include a legal team that deals with negotiating contracts for workers, athletes, and contractors to handle large construction jobs throughout the stadium. The legal team may be small, but they work with a wide variety of departments to deal with all legal issues.

Some of the legal issues that might come before the legal or business offices include compliance with local, state, and national laws. This includes handicapped access within the stadium and making sure all health, safety, and environmental regulations are followed.

These are all of the behind-the-scenes things that come as part of the stadium operations business. A person who decides to move from another field into the area of stadium and sports facility operations can easily do so by moving into office management because it is the area of the business that overlaps most with other kinds of businesses.

EVENT COORDINATOR

An interesting part of stadium management is managing particular events. This kind of job is good for someone who always likes to be met with a new challenge and to have new projects to start up and see through to their end. Event management involves taking care of the details that are involved in making a special event happen at the stadium. These events often go past managing the regular sports season. Plenty of stadiums hold concerts or charity fund-raisers during times when regular season games are not being held. The events raise extra money for the stadium to keep it profitable, and the special events also help promote the stadium. Those extra events require a lot of planning and organization.

An event planner has to have good interpersonal skills and be a great organizer able to work in a fast-paced environment. Problem solving and quick decision-making skills are also a plus for someone who would like to get involved in this area. It can be challenging to organize an event and take care of every small detail. For example, the arrangements would not only include food but all of the utensils, plates, and other details that go into serving food and disposing of it as well. Event planners find the right size room in the stadium to hold the event and must attend to details such as getting the area cleared for public use and making the approaching area presentable to the guests.

If you are interested in event planning, there are certificate programs available and specialty degrees in the area of hospitality and tourism. Online courses are also possible. However, a degree or course may not be necessary if you are willing to learn on the job and work with a supervisor or mentor to learn the business.

SECURITY MANAGER

The security department probably has one of the most important jobs at a large stadium. The work done by this department has a large impact on public safety. With each sporting season, the security at large stadiums increases and policies become tighter to help maintain safety from public dangers such as terrorism and other threats. Policies are put into place to determine what kinds of items the public is allowed to bring into the stadium and what must be confiscated at the door. Security guards in large stadiums routinely search backpacks and ban items that don't pass their criteria as being safe. For example, after the 2013 bombings at the Boston Marathon, security was heightened during other large sporting events. Gillette Stadium in Massachusetts, home of the New England Patriots, stepped up its security restrictions. Its new regulations state that only clear plastic, vinyl, or PVC bags no

Security cameras and monitoring rooms keep large public gatherings safe. These security agents examine security at an MLB All-Star Game and prepare for World Series security.

larger than 12 inches by 6 inches by 12 inches (30 centi-meters by 15 cm by 30 cm) will be allowed to be brought into the stadium. The new policy was made in an attempt to keep homemade bombs off the premises and to keep the public safe. However, that's a strict new policy that will need to be enforced by many security workers at every gate and entrance in the stadium.

The work in a security department can become high-pressured and difficult at times. People who can do these jobs must have strong self-restraint when working with the public, and they must be knowledge-able of all of the security policies of the stadium and know the proper procedure to follow when someone does not adhere to these policies.

Many stadiums hire out security guards from private companies and contractors, and some of these guards work part-time, only during games. The manager oversees these employees and is involved in training them. The manager is also in charge of overseeing emergency exit routes from the stadium from each location and ensuring that surveillance systems such as closed-security cameras are both in place and monitored at all times. A manager may become trained on the job and be promoted within the stadium, or the manager may have a background in security or police work. Each stadium is different in terms of the protection that each security guard receives and how they are permitted to deal with public rowdiness.

The new Jumbotron at Denver's Pepsi Center makes the stadium experience more enjoyable for Colorado Avalanche hockey fans.

Stadiums may contact local police in the event of problems or when stadium patrons have broken the law.

COMMUNICATIONS MANAGER

The communications services at a large stadium are usually very modern and complex. They range from closed-circuit cameras and walkie-talkie systems for the security department to the Jumbotron large-screened television that spectators use to view the game below. The sound systems, broadcast setups, and press and media hookups all fall under the category of communications in a large stadium. Add to that the security control room for monitoring the movement of thousands of people around the stadium and you can see why the communications department is so important to these large facilities.

A person who would work well in a communications department will have a good knowledge of technology and will be willing to keep up on current changes in the field. A manager or supervisor in the department oversees the technicians and system operators and also stays in contact with other departments that are using the equipment.

People in this department may have a background in electronics or engineering. Even if the manager is not a trained technician or engineer, he or she will need to have a working knowledge of how equipment works and know how to troubleshoot if something goes wrong. The communications department may work closely with outside contractors, which are companies that are hired to work for the stadium to perform large jobs, such as replace a Jumbotron, service it, or update a communications or surveillance system in the stadium.

MAINTENANCE MANAGER

The maintenance manager of a large stadium is in charge of keeping the facility operational and

TRANSFORMING A STADIUM

Have you ever seen a football field transform for a dazzling half-time show? In some facilities, a slick basketball court becomes an ice hockey rink in a matter of hours. In other facilities, a baseball field might transform into a concert stage. The transformations that some stadiums go through are amazing. The work of event planners, maintenance, and other departments come together to get the job done. These kinds of events can add excitement to the jobs of the stadium operators.

During the Super Bowl, the field must transform quickly into a performing stage. The 2013 Super Bowl featured Destiny's Child during the halftime show.

presentable. The physical appearance of the stadium is important for making a first impression to the public and media. But even more important, there are safety and health regulations to follow that have to do with the operational condition of a stadium. Stadiums are regularly checked by safety and health inspectors, and the results of the inspections show how well the maintenance department is doing.

Maintenance can be considered cleaning the bathrooms, locker rooms, and kitchens around the stadium. It can also be considered changing lightbulbs or fixing

The Washington Nationals baseball team had a new stadium built in 2007. Here, a machine lays out the final batch of sod on the playing field.

problems with electronics or plumbing. However, the maintenance crew also has a vast working knowledge of the stadium and may be asked to do odd tasks, such as pull a tarp over a baseball field during a rain delay, then neatly drying and storing that tarp for a later use. Maintenance crews are responsible for working complex machinery and equipment, such as ice rink cleaners. They lay down artificial turf on the field, maintain dugout and practice areas, and water and weed all plants and garden areas throughout the stadium. Basically anything you see around a stadium must be regularly maintained. In addition to these daily tasks, they are in charge of the sanitation storage and pickup. This can be a huge job unto itself, as stadiums may have hundreds of trash cans throughout the area of the stands, food services areas, hallways, and offices. Because of the vast amount of work that goes into the facility operations and maintenance, the maintenance department may be broken into many smaller sections, so workers might be able to learn one section well and specialize in it.

A maintenance manager must oversee all of the tasks of the maintenance crew and be able to delegate tasks. A working knowledge is needed of the tools required to do each task, and training of crew members may be necessary. When jobs can't be done by the regular crew, the manager must know how to call in outside help, such as contractors, to get the job done. A maintenance manager should have good leadership qualities and be able to communicate well with staff of all levels.

FOOD SERVICES DIRECTOR

Once people enter the stadium and settle down for hours of enjoyment, they expect to be able to get quality food and beverages. The food services departments are the most profitable for the stadiums. The director of this department oversees all of the food stands, snack counters, and bars, as well as the employees in each of these places. The director works closely with the managers of each food station throughout the stadium, ensuring that they all follow the same rules and regulations. Food safety is an important issue, so strict guidelines about food preparation and service are put in place and must be followed uniformly by each station.

The director oversees the ordering of food and other supplies and keeps up to date with liquor licenses and other state and federal requirements for serving food and alcohol. The guidelines for selling alcohol can be strict, and the penalties for not following the guidelines are serious, so stadiums must be vigilant about selling alcohol only to adults.

Ordering food in large quantities and ensuring safe storage and cooking of the foods is an important task of the food services department. There are many varied

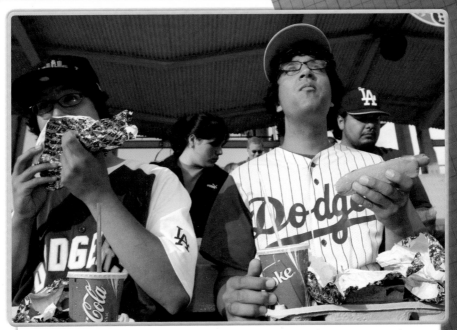

Part of the experience of going to a sports game is enjoying the concessions. These Dodgers fans enjoy hot dogs, nachos, and sodas while they watch their team play.

tasks that go into running the department smoothly. That includes training employees to use the cash registers, interact with the public quickly and efficiently, and deal with special cases when customers have a problem with the food services.

Food services managers may have prior experience in restaurants or in managing food services in other locations. A degree in hospitality and tourism may prepare someone for a food services career and so can online classes or certificates in food services. A person who can excel in this kind of career path at a stadium must be detail-oriented and know a lot about the regulations of the food industry.

SALES COORDINATOR

Without ticket sales, a stadium could not stay in business long. A sales department is responsible for setting ticket prices, making them available through certain ticket outlets, and setting up promotions and group sales rates. A sales coordinator may be responsible for getting a certain quota of tickets sold each season to guarantee that the

STADIUM PRIDE

Working in a large sports stadium on a daily basis may be exciting and enjoyable for sports fans. Many employees at the stadiums are in fact fans of the teams that play there. They may have grown up around the general area and known that stadium well as a child. They may also just be sports fans who are looking for an opportunity to work in a professional sports environment. But once they begin working at the stadium, a sense of pride in the team may develop. Stadium workers may find themselves aligned and loyal to the team that plays there just as much as they are with the operations of the physical stadium that the team plays in.

stadium will have the expected income it needs to make a profit on its operations. Some sales coordinators have training in sales, or they may have a certificate or degree in sales or business.

The personality of a sales coordinator must be strong and detail-oriented. Good communication skills are necessary, and a friendly, likeable persona must be portrayed to the public. Sales coordinators may work closely with business offices, but they have a presence in the public areas of the stadium as well.

MEDIA RELATIONS

There is usually a strong media presence at any professional sports game. The games are broadcast on television, on the Internet, and over the radio. Members of the press have special VIP boxes that allow them to comfortably watch the game while organizing the information they need to write and report about the game. The job of the media relations or other similar department at the stadium is to keep the media comfortable and satisfied. Media teams representing the visiting teams are also put in touch with the media relations department to find a comfortable area from which to broadcast or work.

The media relations department works somewhat like a public relations department. It is the connection between the media and the stadium. It is concerned with

Professional soccer player Thierry Henry of the New York Red Bulls is fitted with a microphone before an interview at Crew Stadium in Columbus, Ohio.

having the stadium and team look good, and it works to make the stadium an inviting place to broadcast from.

In order for the media to have the correct access to the stadium, they need to feel comfortable and welcome in press boxes and media broadcast areas. They need access to locker rooms to conduct interviews with athletes. They need access to the sidelines or the dugout areas to conduct interviews and give reports. That means working closely with the security department to make sure that athletes and coaches are safe and that the general public does not gain access to areas where they should not be. The media broadcasting areas must be well-organized and clean and have the right communications hookups.

This department might also work with a legal adviser to work out contracts with broadcasting companies for the rights to broadcast the games on their stations or networks. Someone who works with the media should have excellent communication skills and be able to think creatively to solve problems. Special education requirements might include classes in business or media or a degree in business.

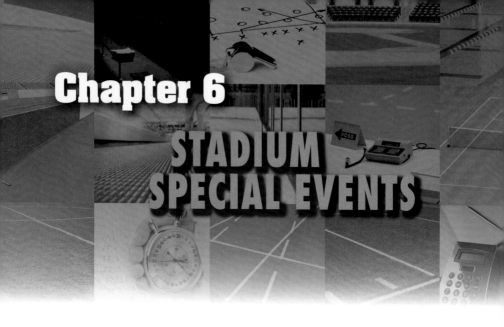

Chapter 6
STADIUM SPECIAL EVENTS

The growth of the sports industry has increased steadily over the past several decades, and about three hundred universities around the United States offer degrees in sports management. However, in a slow economy, jobs can be hard to find. It helps to keep options open and to look for as many opportunities as possible. The wide variety of special events that occur at large stadiums can provide great opportunities for people to get experience with events while they may not have a regular, full-time job at a stadium.

Play-off games, Super Bowl games, and concerts are large events with high public profile and extensive media coverage. Such events bring in millions of dollars, and the details of their organization are massive. Large events such as the Super Bowl and the Olympics have permanent organizing committees in place to plan the events years in advance.

SUPER BOWL

The Super Bowl is such a huge event that it is planned by organized committees years ahead of time. The location of the Super Bowl is chosen well in advance because extensive planning takes place to get the stadium ready. Then, just weeks before, play-off and championship games decide which teams will have the honor of playing at that stadium for the Super Bowl.

The permanent planning committee will start its journey by first collecting bids from stadiums that wish to host the Super Bowl. The bid may include details about what they plan to do during the event and how they expect to handle the extra crowds. When a venue is chosen for a particular year, the committee starts fund-raising to earn money for the event. Then, volunteers from the public are asked to join in to help.

Most Super Bowls are held in indoor stadiums so that they can be held no matter what the weather is. That said, the winning bid for the February 2, 2014, Super Bowl XLVIII went to the non-domed MetLife Stadium, home of the New York Giants and New York Jets. It's the only National Football League (NFL) stadium shared equally by two teams. The football teams worked together to have the new stadium built in 2010. A month after it was opened, it was announced that it would host the 2014 Super Bowl.

MetLife Stadium in East Rutherford, New Jersey, houses two professional football teams and was the host of the XLVIII Super Bowl.

The stadium itself is in East Rutherford, New Jersey, so the event was advertised as being hosted by both New York and New Jersey. It was the first time the Super Bowl was played in an open, outdoor stadium in a cold-weather city. The usual requirements of the Super Bowl hosting

stadium state that the average temperatures of the hosting city must be at least fifty degrees Fahrenheit (ten degrees Celsius) if it wishes to host in an outdoor stadium. New Jersey winters are much colder than that, but the requirement was waived by the NFL commissioner, Roger Goodell. The hosting opportunity was allowed on the ballot and won the hosting position because it would be a once-only event that could help to celebrate the heritage and history of New York.

Staging an event such as a Super Bowl takes massive amounts of planning. Booking a halftime show is a challenge in and of itself. The biggest names in entertainment are considered to play at the event, and much consideration goes into figuring out exactly whom that should be. Then, planning *how* the stadium will be transformed from a football field to an extravagant stage show arena and *back* into a football field in less than thirty minutes must be worked out to the smallest detail. Many halftime shows include complex audio, video, and pyrotechnic aspects, and a large number of performers put on the show. Specialists in different areas must work out how to plan and execute the building of the stages, the wiring of sound and cameras, and the breaking down of equipment so that the show will not extend too long so that the football game can continue on time. There must be areas for the performers to get ready so that they are not in the way of the athletes, coaches, or fans.

There are other concerns besides the halftime show. Security in a Super Bowl arena must be among the tightest of any public event. Security checks, restrictions of personal items, and good communications are needed throughout the stadium to ensure public safety. Food vendors must be vigilant about the alcohol being sold so that public rowdiness can be kept to a minimum.

The Super Bowl is such an anticipated event partly because it determines the championship team for the season, but also because it is highly publicized and covered by the media. The broadcasting areas at the Super Bowl must be the most professional and well planned of the football season. The game is broadcast on network television as well as through other broadcast mediums, such as cable, Internet, and radio. Broadcasting booths are used so that announcers can give play-by-play descriptions as well as conduct interviews during the game. Areas are even set up near locker rooms for interviews and media access.

The Super Bowl creates a frenzy of events for people working in sports. Inside Edition's Katherine Webb interviews Pernell McPhee (left) and DeAngelo Tyson of the Baltimore Ravens during Super Bowl XLVII in 2013.

The broadcasting of the three- or four-hour event takes years to organize so that it can be executed smoothly, safely, and successfully. As the event gets closer, the planning goes into high gear as more and more vendors and broadcasters are decided upon. They are given extensive regulations to follow in order to keep their status as a Super Bowl contributor.

SUPER BOWL VOLUNTEERS

Working for the Super Bowl planning committee may seem like an advanced job in the world of stadium operations. After all, it is the most publicized and anticipated event of the football season. Just one thirty-second commercial during the game costs millions of dollars to air because of the huge viewership. However, there are opportunities for volunteers to help the hosting committee. The Super Bowl XLVIII committee for the New York and New Jersey Super Bowl used over fifteen thousand volunteers to help prepare for the game. The volunteers did not work in the stadium during the game, but they worked as greeters to guests coming into airport terminals, train stations, and other transportation areas. They volunteered at hotels and other tourist locations to provide information to visitors about the area and to answer questions. The volunteers were local residents who knew the area well and could make supporters of both teams feel welcome. They were also present at other promotional events that led up to the games. The volunteers went to at least one training session related to their assignment, and they worked a minimum of two shifts of three to four hours each. All volunteers helped during the pregame events and times. During the game itself, only professional, trained staff was used.

OLYMPIC GAMES

The Olympic Games are probably the most complex sporting event to organize. The worldwide sporting competition involves 204 recognized nations that compete in twenty-six sports. In 2016, that number will increase to twenty-eight. The games have been held since 1896, and they keep getting more and more complex in terms of their planning, organization, and execution.

The Olympic Games are presided over by the International Olympic Committee, then are divided into five continental associations, and then further divided into each National Olympic Committee. The committees make sure that their nation and athletes follow the extensive requirements for play and participation. But that's only one part of the planning that goes into the events. The International Olympic Committee is also involved in choosing the locations where future Olympics will be held. The host city that is chosen will have a guaranteed boost to its economy as well as a publicity boost. Thousands of people will descend upon the city to watch and cover the games, and that city must be ready.

In most cases, the host city must have multiple stadiums planned and built to house the different events. Summer Olympic cities must have large arenas for track and field events, swimming and diving, gymnastics, and many other competitive sports, such as baseball,

The London Olympics Opening Ceremony in 2012 required coordination of a large number of specialists working in security, communications, and customer service.

tennis, weight-lifting, and cycling. Some cities even need to have hotels, roads, or restaurants built to handle the large number of people who will use the facilities and area infrastructure for the two-week event. A large arena is also needed for opening and closing events, which are even more intricately planned and detailed than Super Bowl halftime shows. On the first day of the opening ceremonies, a parade of athletes from every competing nation is put on, as well as a stage show by the host country, showcasing its culture and history. The opening ceremonies may be hours long, and they are televised around the world. Commentators in every language and from every country broadcast from the events, making it a truly international as well as a truly complex event to host.

People specializing in sports facility and stadium operations must be hired at each of the facilities. Security, communications, food services, information, and every other detail is necessary to make the events run smoothly. Even though the jobs are temporary, Olympic workers do the same kinds of jobs that stadium workers do. People who know different languages are especially valuable to an Olympic committee who hires workers. The mix of people from different countries and who speak different languages is one of the things that makes the Olympics such a special event. The convergence of cultures for the common sake of celebrating and competing in sports makes the Olympics a unique experience. The athletes who train their whole lives provide inspiration to the spectators who watch in person as well as those who watch throughout the world in their homes.

The skills that are required for people to work in sports facilities such as swim clubs or exercise facilities are needed at the Olympic Games as well. These workers keep swimming pools in excellent operational order and make sure gymnastics or track and field equipment is working well and being stored properly.

As with the days leading up to the Super Bowl, Olympic hosting cities use the volunteer help of local citizens to help give information to visiting spectators so that they feel welcome. The coordination of numerous events can be difficult, but people with event planning experience can excel in the planning stages to help ensure that the day-to-day operations during the games run smoothly. Once planning is complete, the security, communications, and maintenance crews take over to help ensure smooth operations.

A POLITICAL GAME

Although the Olympics are meant to be an international event of goodwill and sportsmanship, the games *can* become political because of the wide range of nations involved. Ideally, the Olympics should be a time when political differences are put aside and people come to watch world-class athletes perform on a world stage. The athletes involved have trained nearly their whole lives to get to the Olympic Games. Nonetheless, once in a while a worldwide political event may cause some countries to boycott the games. The 1980 Summer Olympics in Moscow were boycotted by the United States, Canada, and many other countries to protest the Soviet invasion of Afghanistan. The next Summer Olympic Games, held in Los Angeles, were boycotted by the Soviet Union and thirteen of its allies. Such political moves hurt the athletes of the boycotting countries and their families, as they negate the athletes' sacrifices and efforts; they will be unable to see how they would have performed and whether they could have brought home those medals for which they worked so hard.

For the most part, however, countries put aside their political differences to celebrate their own athletes and compete in the sporting tradition. The games provide inspiration to young athletes, providing a good example of dedication, sportsmanship, and physical fitness. In the 2012 London Olympic Games, there were even four athletes who competed as independent athletes. They were athletes with no nation to represent them. One Olympic marathon athlete, Guor Marial, was a refugee from the Sudanese civil war, which took the lives of many of his family members. He refused to run on behalf of the Sudanese and considers himself South Sudanese, even though the new nation has not yet formed an Olympic committee. The marathon runner lived in the United States and even had trouble getting a passport to get him to London in time to compete in the games.

Athletes who compete without a country can be a great reminder of the importance of the Olympic Games for bringing nations together in one venue and for one purpose—to celebrate sporting and competition.

South Sudanese runner Guor Marial competed in the 2012 London Olympics men's marathon as an independent athlete. The refugee chose not to represent Sudan but to run independently.

CHOOSING A CITY

The process of choosing a city to host the Olympic Games can be complex and take several years. First, cities that wish to host the games apply on a regional level. For example, American cities would compete against each other to be considered by the International Olympic Committee. It could be Chicago, Denver, and Los Angeles all competing for the regional consideration. Each city describes why it would be the best choice and how it would accommodate the events. Previous experience in hosting sporting events is helpful in convincing the committee that one's city is ready. Large events such as World Cup finals, large cycling events, or Super Bowl games can help show that a given city has been successful in the past. The regional level choices are made through voting, and the winner is then considered for the international level evaluations.

At the international level, just a few cities are left for consideration. The final evaluation that resulted in choosing Rio de Janeiro, Brazil, for the 2016 Summer Games meant that the other finalists—Madrid, Spain; Chicago, Illinois; and Tokyo, Japan—were eliminated.

Before the final voting, each city makes a one-hour presentation to the committee that might include speeches, promotional videos, and celebrity endorsements. Then 105 members of the International Olympic Committee vote by secret ballot to decide who should win. The voting is repeated until one city is left with the majority of votes. If a member lives in one of the participating countries, that member cannot vote until his or her home country has been eliminated from the consideration.

When a city decides to go through the process of bidding to host the Olympic Games, it must put a lot of time and money into the process. The cities that make it to the final round of voting put in about $40 million to set up their presentations and make detailed plans. If the city does not win, the money is lost and there is no recognition for its efforts. The city that wins must then spend billions more to make its plans a reality. However, a hosting city gets an enormous amount of publicity through television coverage and corporate sponsorship advertising. The city may not make back all of the money that it spent bidding for, hosting, and promoting the games, but it will certainly boost its presence on the world stage.

The construction in the hosting city also helps to permanently boost the economy of the area. For example, after the 1980 Winter Olympic Games were held in Lake Placid, New York, the facilities were left standing, but quiet. The ski slopes and Olympic stadium are now used year-round as sporting facilities. Athletes are trained there, and Olympic hopefuls continue to go to competitive events where the Olympic Games were once held. Tourists are invited to visit the training facilities and watch athletes perform on the ski slopes all year long. An Olympic museum helps

DESIGNING AN OLYMPIC STADIUM

The 2014 Winter Olympic Games in Sochi, Russia, were a perfect opportunity for stadium designers to build a magnificent structure. The Fisht Olympic Stadium inside the Sochi Olympic Park is that kind of magnificent structure. The 40,000-seat stadium is strategically placed on Fisht Mountain, a snowy mountain whose name means "white head" or "white frost." At 9,373 feet (2,857 m) above sea level, the mountain provides a unique backdrop for the stadium, and architects worked the

Russia spent millions to accommodate the 2014 Winter Olympics in Sochi. The Fisht Olympic Stadium is one of the crowning accomplishments of the preparations.

mountain scenery into the design of the stadium. The sides of the roof are made of a translucent polycarbonate material that makes the building look like it is part of the snowy peaks that surround it. The very top of the stadium roof is completely transparent. This gives the spectators inside the stadium a complete view of the whole mountain from its foot to its peak. The stadium will be used for the opening and closing ceremonies, as well as for medal ceremonies. When the Olympic Games are over, Fisht Stadium will be used as a soccer stadium and for hosting special sporting and entertainment events. The stadium will appear bright from the inside because of the transparent and translucent areas of the roof. The stadium will be an addition to the region and the country for years to come.

to attract tourists to the Adirondack Mountains to stop in the small city for a visit.

QUICK CONSTRUCTION

Just as the 2012 Summer Olympic Games were ending in London, England, construction was beginning for the 2014 Winter Olympic Games in Sochi, Russia. Over 96,000 workers began laboring away for over 500 companies that were hired to do contract work and construction to get the Olympic Games ready. The small city of 345,000 people was transformed in many ways. In addition to the stadiums and ski jump facilities, new roads were built and twenty-two tunnels dug. The work also included building hotels, high-rise apartment buildings, sidewalks, power plants, and train stations, and laying miles of railroad tracks. Eight power plants and a new electricity power grid replaced the older, less-powerful system of electric supply.

While some places such as London are already equipped for large crowds and have modern transportation and arenas for gathering, the Olympic committees like to present the games as an international cultural event. They choose diverse locations around the world, which means that some more rural areas need to be quickly modernized to handle the events. People who are interested in working in the field of sports facilities and sports events could benefit greatly by working as a volunteer or part-time worker to prepare for one of these events.

PREPARING FOR A CAREER

Not everyone is lucky enough to be able to have a large sporting event roll into their town, so doing a little digging and looking around for opportunities is a good idea. Check sports journals for articles about new contracts for upcoming events near you. Then check newspaper

Preparing for a career in sports facility or stadium operations means preparing for an interview. Even volunteers and interns must make a good impression on a potential employer.

classified listings closer to the time of the event that indicate what kind of help is needed. Any opportunity can get you closer to the event experience and lead to a unique job that can be listed on a résumé. Volunteering to prepare for an event is a great way to "get in on the ground floor" and meet new people who may be able to help your career later.

During future job interviews you may have in the field of sports facilities or stadiums, your volunteer work will be a great source of discussion. You will have a chance to prove that you showed initiative and got involved as a volunteer. This can cause an employer to choose you over others who have not had that same experience.

Any preparation for a large sporting event is valuable experience, even if it is not for an Olympic event or a championship game. A person will use the same skills to prepare for a special one-time event as he or she would to work in sports facility or stadium operations. Some people even focus on special-event planning as a career. These people may have special skills in renting out arenas for a particular event and working as an event planner. No matter what your focus is in the field of stadium and sports facility operations, you can be proud that you pursued a career in something that you have always loved—sports.

COLLEGE AND UNIVERSITY PROGRAMS IN SPORTS MANAGEMENT

The following is a list of colleges and universities that offer undergraduate programs in sports management.

Adams State College
Alamosa, Colorado
Programs of study: sports
   management, bachelor's
   and master's level

Alfred State College
Alfred, New York
Programs of study: sports
   management, bachelor's
   level

Bellevue University
Bellevue, Nebraska
Programs of study: sports
   management, bachelor's
   level

Campbell University
Buies Creek, North Carolina
Programs of study: sports
   management, bachelor's
   level

Clemson University
Clemson, South Carolina
Programs of study: sports
   management, bachelor's
   level

Florida State University
Tallahassee, Florida
Programs of study: sports
   management, bachelor's
   and master's level

Georgia Southern University
Statesboro, Georgia
Programs of study: sports
   management, bachelor's
   and master's level

Indiana State University
Terre Haute, Indiana
Programs of study: sports
   management, bachelor's
   and master's level

Kent State University
Kent, Ohio
Programs of study: sports
management, bachelor's and
master's level

Kutztown University
Kutztown, Pennsylvania
Programs of study: sports
management, bachelor's
level

Loyola University
Chicago, Illinois
Programs of study: sports
management, bachelor's and
master's level

Marian College
Indianapolis, Indiana
Programs of study: sports
management, bachelor's
level

Nichols College
Dudley, Massachusetts
Programs of study: sports
management, bachelor's
level

Southern Illinois University
Carbondale, Illinois
Programs of study: sports
management, bachelor's and
master's level

Troy University
Troy, Alabama
Programs of study: sports
management, bachelor's and
master's level

Western Carolina University
Cullowhee, North Carolina
Programs of study: sports
management, bachelor's
level

A CAREER IN SPORTS FACILITY OPERATIONS AT A GLANCE

COMMUNICATIONS MANAGER

ACADEMICS

- High school graduate
- Bachelor's degree
- Certificate, associate's degree, or equivalent

EXPERIENCE

- Internships at sports facilities or stadiums.
- Entry-level positions as mechanics or technology specialists.
- Coordinator positions help determine the communication needs of other departments.

CAREER PATHS

- Employees may work in large or small venues.

- Some employees may be promoted from within a company, moving from a service position to a managerial position.

- Some employees may receive extra training outside the job to keep up on new technologies.

DUTIES AND RESPONSIBILITIES

- Connect and/or repair communication devices in sports stadiums or facilities.

- Communicate with other departments about their communication needs.

- Work closely with security department to install and monitor security cameras.

- Set up and maintain wireless communication systems throughout a stadium or facility.

EVENT SECURITY SPECIALIST

ACADEMICS

- High school diploma
- Bachelor's degree optional
- Tactical training
- Security specialist certification training

EXPERIENCE

- Physical security training—on the job or through certification
- Firearms training and certification possible
- Law enforcement training possible
- Security guard training

CAREER PATHS

- Some security specialists have their own security business.
- Some specialists become consultants who specialize in security loopholes.
- Manage a security team.
- Can also work in security at large events, night clubs, restaurants, retail, or corporations.

DUTIES AND RESPONSIBILITIES

- Secure areas and capture suspects when necessary
- Develop emergency exits and procedures to put in place in the event of crisis situations
- Keep public safe

OFFICE MANAGER

ACADEMICS

- High school diploma
- Possible associate's degree
- Possible business certificate
- Possible bachelor's degree in business administration

EXPERIENCE

- Performing business duties related to running an office
- Knowledge of accounting, finance, technology possible

CAREER PATHS

- Office managers can work in almost any field.

- Some office managers at stadiums or facilities may learn a specialty related to the sports field, such as sports management or sports marketing.

- Some office managers may work closely with lawyers, broadcasting professionals, or even athletes or coaches.

DUTIES AND RESPONSIBILITIES

- Present a professional attitude and atmosphere to clients

- Perform detail-oriented tasks such as filing of hard copy and digital files, typing, writing letters, and taking accurate notes in meetings

- Understand accounting or financial details related to the sports business, such as ticket or food prices, and details related to building contracts or regulations

CONSTRUCTION MANAGER

SIGNIFICANT POINTS

- Many construction managers work long, irregular hours.

- Competition with other construction firms for work on sports facilities can be quite intense.

- Construction managers at sports facilities work closely with architects and sports facility managers throughout a construction project.

NATURE OF THE WORK

Construction managers plan, budget, coordinate, and supervise construction projects from early development to completion.

TRAINING

Formal requirements include a four-year bachelor's degree in a construction-related field or work experience in a construction trade. Certification is encouraged.

OTHER QUALIFICATIONS

In addition to their knowledge of construction, plumbing, and electrical work, construction managers also spend time in offices working on the business aspect of the job. Large projects such as sports facilities are often handled by very large construction firms.

ADVANCEMENT

Approximately two-thirds of construction managers are self-employed and may work with a sports facility on a contract basis. The advancement of the management company may be based on a portfolio of past work and on reputation.

JOB OUTLOOK

The construction manager field is expected to grow 17 percent from 2010 to 2020, about average for all occupations. Candidates with a degree in a construction-related field have the best outlook for employment and advancement.

WORK ENVIRONMENT

The work environment includes both office and outdoor work at construction sites. There are considerable dangers to working at construction sites, and training is paramount to staying safe on the job.

EVENT PLANNER

SIGNIFICANT POINTS

- Event planners coordinate all aspects of professional meetings and events.

- They choose meeting locations, arrange transportation for guests or other important meeting members, and coordinate all details pertaining to the event.

- Event planners may work long hours, especially right before a planned event takes place.

NATURE OF THE WORK

The work of an event planner in the sports field can be fast-paced and highly competitive and may involve high-profile guests.

TRAINING

Many event planners have an associate's or bachelor's degree in hospitality management. They must learn on the job through extensive experience planning events of all sizes.

OTHER QUALIFICATIONS

People who wish to be event planners must be prepared to do detailed planning and pay special attention to details such as communication with guests. Contacts in the food service and transportation business are a plus.

ADVANCEMENT

Event planners may form their own business after they have gained experience in the field, where they may do contract work to plan events. Large stadiums may have advancement within the field for large events such as a Super Bowl or play-off games.

JOB OUTLOOK

Employment of event planners is expected to grow 44 percent from 2010 to 2020, which is much faster than average for all occupations. Job outlook is best for those with a bachelor's degree in a related field, such as hospitality management.

WORK ENVIRONMENT

Most of the work of event planners is done in an office environment. During the event, the work is on-site, such as at hotels, convention centers, stadiums, or sport facilities. Event planners may travel to visit and appraise prospective meeting sites.

OFFICE ASSISTANT

SIGNIFICANT POINTS

- Many office assistants work long hours but are not expected to work hours as long as their managers.

- Office assistants are trained in managing office details, including filing, computer work, and communication and organization.

NATURE OF THE WORK

Work in a stadium or sports facility office may be fast-paced and require quick and accurate responses to and from other departments with whom the assistant is communicating.

TRAINING

Most office assistants have no more than an associate's degree and are not required to have an associate's degree to do the work. An office assistant may be an entry-level job for someone who wishes to rise in the company and learn more about the business from within.

OTHER QUALIFICATIONS

Office assistants must be very detail-oriented and accurate in their work. They must take direction well and be professional in their demeanor.

ADVANCEMENT

An office assistant may be promoted to office coordinator, and eventually office manager. Advancement within a company depends, among other factors, on the years and quality of experience.

JOB OUTLOOK

Employment of office assistants is expected to grow 10 percent from 2010 to 2020, about as fast as the average for all occupations.

WORK ENVIRONMENT

The work environment in a sports stadium or facility may be more open or casual than that of a corporate office. The majority of work is full-time.

GLOSSARY

accounting Action or process of keeping financial records.

arena A place where a sporting event takes place, usually on a large scale.

associate's degree Post–high school level degree that usually requires two years of study.

bachelor's degree Post–high school level degree that usually requires four years of study.

boycott To refuse to take part in buying a product or attending an event.

business management Degree or career focus that concentrates on business leadership, problem solving, or critical thinking.

certificate Official document that attests that a certain level of achievement or study has been completed.

commissioner Person appointed to regulate a particular sport.

contract A legal document that sets forth the terms of an agreement between two or more parties.

customer service The assistance and advice provided by a company about its products or services.

event management The organization of a professional event.

event planning Part of the hospitality industry dedicated to planning and coordinating large events, often for the public or corporations.

human resources Department in a professional business that focuses on hiring, firing, or training employees.

International Olympic Committee Committee that plans Olympic Games on an international level, coordinating events with committees at a national level.

internship A paid or unpaid entry-level position that is meant for training purposes and may provide school credits.

Jumbotron The large screen at most sports arenas that broadcasts the game or performance so all spectators at the arena can see it.

marketing The action or business of promoting or selling products or services.

master's degree Academic postgraduate degree.

mentor An experienced and trusted adviser.

National Olympic Committee A committee from one of the 204 nations participating in the Olympic Games.

NFL National Football League; professional American football league consisting of the National Football Conference and the American Football Conference.

office manager Person who is responsible for the daily operations of a business, including managing its staff.

security The organized department or professional field responsible for keeping the public safe from harm at large public events such as sporting events.

sports facility Term used to describe businesses or buildings dedicated to sports and fitness for public use.

sports management Field of the sporting industry dedicated to the business of sports and the coordination of sporting events.

sports marketing Field of the sporting industry dedicated to the business of sports and the promotion of sports.

sports stadium A large facility dedicated to professional sports games and equipped with thousands of seats for spectator viewing.

Super Bowl Annual championship game of the National Football League.

violation The act of breaking a rule or formal agreement or not complying with regulations.

volunteer One who works without pay.

World Series Annual championship series played between the two leagues in American professional baseball.

FOR MORE INFORMATION

Canada Sport Institute
204-12 Concorde Place
Toronto, ON M3C 3R8
Canada
(416) 426-7238
Web site: http://csiontario.ca
The Canada Sport Institute is a member of a network of
  institutes dedicated to enhancing the daily training
  environment of Canada's athletes and coaches.

Canadian Olympic Committee
4141 Pier-de-Coubertin
Montreal, QC H1V 3N7
Canada
(514) 861-3371
Web site: http://olympic.ca
The Canadian Olympic Committee is an organization that
  tracks the Olympic records and activities of Canadian
  athletes participating in Olympic Games.

International Sports Federation
Chateau de Vidy
Case postale 356
1001 Lausanne
Switzerland
Web site: http://www.olympic.org
This international, nonprofit agency monitors the way many
  international sports disciplines are recognized, regu-
  lated, and played.

North American Society for Sports Management
15 Winterwood Drive
Butler, PA 16001
(724) 482-6277
Web site: http://www.nassm.com
This organization promotes study and research in the field
of sports management, including job outlooks in the
field.

Sport Business Research Network
P.O. Box 2378
Princeton, NJ 08543
(609) 896-1996
Web site: http://www.sbrnet.com
This group assists individuals or organizations interested in
sports-related issues, such as market research, govern-
ment statistics, lawsuit records, and reports about sports
facilities and venues.

The Sports Facility Advisory
600 Cleveland Street, Suite 910
Clearwater, FL 33755
(727) 474-3845
Web site: http://www.sportadvisory.com
The Sports Facility Advisory provides services to new and
existing sport and recreation center operators.

Sportsplex Operators and Developers Association
P.O. Box 24263—Westgate Station
Rochester, NY 14624-0263
(585) 426-2215
Web site: http://www.sportsplexoperators.com
The organization is devoted to providing a venue for sports
facility owners and operators to exchange experiences
and ideas through discussion, study, and publications.

U.S. Indoor Sports Association
1340 N. Great Neck Road, Suite 1272-142
Virginia Beach, VA 23454
(509) 357-7096
Web site: http://www.usindoor.com
The U.S. Indoor Sports Association serves the needs of
multisport facilities, including startup companies.
It provides referrals for builders and sport facility
equipment.

U.S. National Olympic Committee
1 Olympic Plaza
Colorado Springs, CO 80909
(719) 632-5551
Web site: http://www.teamusa.org
This organization tracks the Olympic records and activi-
ties of American athletes participating in the Olympic
Games.

WEB SITES

Due to the changing nature of Internet links, Rosen
Publishing has developed an online list of Web sites related
to the subject of this book. This site is updated regularly.
Please use this link to access the list:

http://www.rosenlinks.com/GCSI/Stad

FOR FURTHER READING

American Kinesiology Association. *Careers in Sport, Fitness, and Exercise.* Champaign, IL: Human Kinetics, 2011.

Ammon, Robin, Jr. *Sports Facility Management: Organizing Events and Mitigating Risks.* Morgantown, WV: Fitness Information Technology, 2003.

Carfagna, Peter A. *Representing the Professional Athlete* (American Casebook). St. Paul, MN: West, 2009.

Davis, John A. *The Olympic Games Effect: How Sports Marketing Builds Strong Brands.* Hoboken, NJ: Wiley, 2012.

Dell, Donald. *Never Make the First Offer (Except When You Should): Wisdom from a Master Dealmaker.* New York, NY: Portfolio Hardcover, 2009.

Easterbrook, Gregg. *The King of Sports: Football's Impact on America.* New York, NY: Thomas Dunne Books, 2013.

Falk, David. *The Bald Truth: Secrets of Success from the Locker Room to the Boardroom.* New York, NY: Gallery Books, 2010.

Field, Shelly. *Career Opportunities in the Sports Industry.* New York, NY: Checkmark Books, 2010.

Fried, Gil. *Managing Sport Facilities.* Champaign, IL: Human Kinetics, 2009.

Gold, John R., and Margaret M. Gold. *Olympic Cities: Agendas, Planning, and the World's Games. 1896–2016.* New York, NY: Routledge, 2010.

Horne, John, and Garry Whannel. *Understanding the Olympics.* New York, NY: Routledge, 2011.

Irwin, Richard L. *Sport Promotion and Sales Management.* Champaign, IL: Human Kinetics, 2008.

Kassens-Noor, Eva. *Planning Olympic Legacies: Transport Dreams and Urban Realities.* New York, NY: Routledge, 2012.

Masteralexis, Lisa P., Carol A. Barr, and Mary Hums. *Principles and Practice of Sport Management.* Burlington, MA: Jones and Bartlett Learning, 2012.

Masterman, Guy. *Strategic Sports Event Management.* 2nd ed. Boston, MA: Elsevier Butterworth-Heinemann, 2009.

Pedersen, Paul, M. Janet Parks, and Jerome Quarterman. *Contemporary Sport Management.* Champaign, IL: Human Kinetics, 2010.

Rosenhaus, Drew, and Jason Rosenhaus. *Next Question: An NFL Super Agent's Proven Game Plan for Business Success.* New York, NY: Berkley Trade, 2009.

Rosenhaus, Drew, and Don Yaeger. *A Shark Never Sleeps: Wheeling and Dealing with the NFL's Most Ruthless Agent.* New York, NY: Atria Books, 1998.

Rosner, Scott, and Kenneth Shropshire. *The Business of Sports.* 2nd ed. Burlington, MA: Jones and Bartlett Learning, 2010.

St. John, Allen. *The Billion Dollar Game: Behind the Scenes of the Greatest Day in American Sport.* New York, NY: Anchor Books, 2010.

Wells, Michelle, Andy Kreutzer, and Jim Kahler. *A Career in Sports: Advice from Sports Business Leaders.* Livonia, MI: M. Wells Enterprises, 2010.

Wong, Glenn M. *The Comprehensive Guide to Careers in Sports*. Burlington, MA: Jones and Bartlett Learning, 2012.

SPORTS JOURNALS

Journal of Sports & Social Issues

Seton Hall Journal of Sports & Entertainment

Sports Business Journal

University of Miami Entertainment & Sports Law Review

Belson, Ken. "In Sports Business, Too Many Hopefuls for
Too Few Positions." *New York Times*, May 26, 2009.
Retrieved July 22, 2013 (http://www.nytimes
.com/2009/05/27/sports/27class.html?_r=0).

CareerStructure.com. "Facilities Manager Job
Description." Retrieved July 8, 2013 (http://www
.careerstructure.com/careers-advice/profiles/
facilities-manager).

Decker, Fred. "Business Administration and Business
Management: The Difference Between Degrees."
Retrieved July 12, 2013 (http://classroom.synonym.
com/business-administration-business
-management-difference-between-degrees-4415
.html).

Fletcher, Dan. "How Is the Olympic Host City Chosen?"
Time.com, October 1, 2009. Retrieved August 1, 2013
(http://www.time.com/time/world/article/
0,8599,1927402,00.html).

Job Monkey. "Professional Sports Jobs: Stadium
Operations Jobs." Retrieved July 20, 2013 (http://
www.jobmonkey.com/sports/html/pro_stadium
_operation.html).

Lake Placid/Essex County Convention and Visitors
Bureau. "Olympic Center and Lake Placid
Olympic Museum." Retrieved August 1, 2013
(http://www.lakeplacid.com/do/family-fun/
olympic-center-and-lake-placid-olympic-museum).

Lally, Kathy. "In Sochi, Olympic Construction to Be
Endured." *The Bulletin*, February 20, 2013. Retrieved

August 1, 2013 (http://www.bendbulletin.com/
   article/20130220/NEWS0107/302200359/).

Lawyue, Matthew. "Careers in Sports Management."
   Bloomsberg Businessweek. Retrieved July
   8, 2013 (http://images.businessweek.com/
   ss/08/08/0818_sports_management).

Monster.com. "Office Manager Job Description."
   Retrieved July 8, 2013 (http://hiring.monster.com/
   hr/hr-best-practices/recruiting-hiring-advice/
   job-descriptions/office-manager-job-description
   -sample.aspx).

Morgan Bolton, Michele. "Security Levels Tighten
   at Gillette Stadium." *Boston Globe,* June 30, 2013.
   Retrieved July 24, 2013 (http://www.bostonglobe
   .com/metro/regionals/south/2013/06/29/
   foxborough-nfl-stepping-security-procedures
   -gillette-stadium/4E7MOSocgkh2twA3wAaenI/
   story.html).

National Association for Sport and Physical Education.
   "Fields of Study—Sports Management." Retrieved
   July 8, 2013 (http://www.aahperd.org/naspe/careers/
   sportmgmt.cfm).

Petchesky, Barry. "There Are Four Olympic Athletes
   Without Countries to Represent." Deadspin, July
   30, 2012. Retrieved August 1, 2013 (http://deadspin.
   com/5930062/there-are-four-olympic-athletes
   -without-countries-to-represent).

Political Geography Now. "Parade of Nations: Which
   Countries Are (and Aren't) in the Olympics?" July 26,
   2012. Retrieved August 1, 2013 (http://www
   .polgeonow.com/2012/07/olympics-parade-of
   -nations.html).

Prospects. "Facilities Manager Job Description."
   Retrieved July 8, 2013 (http://www.prospects.ac.uk/
   facilities_manager_job_description.htm).

Schrotenboer, Brent. "*USA Today* Sports Investigation: Holes in Stadium Security." *USA Today*, May 2, 2013. Retrieved July 22, 2013 (http://www.usatoday.com/story/sports/2013/05/02/stadium-security-boston-marathon-kentucky-derby/2130875).

Sochi.ru. "Fisht Olympic Stadium." Retrieved August 1, 2013 (http://www.sochi2014.com/en/games/places/objects/sea/central_stadium).

Super Bowl XLVIII. "Why Volunteer?" Retrieved August 1, 2013 (http://www.nynjsuperbowl.com/volunteer).

Turner Construction. "Sporting Park." Retrieved July 14, 2013 (http://www.turnerconstruction.com/experience/project/612/sporting-park).

Turner Construction. "Yankee Stadium." Retrieved July 14, 2013 (http://www.turnerconstruction.com/experience/project/1573/yankee-stadium).

Turner Construction. "Yankee Stadium Food & Beverage." Retrieved July 14, 2013 (http://www.turnerconstruction.com/experience/project/1579/yankee-stadium-food-beverage).

UC Berkeley Extension. "Certificate Program in Business Administration." Retrieved July 20, 2013 (http://extension.berkeley.edu/public/category/courseCategoryCertificateProfile.do?method=load&certificateId=17105).

U.S. Energy Information Administration. "Stadiums and Arenas Use Efficient, High Wattage Lamps." Today in Energy. Retrieved July 8, 2013 (http://www.eia.gov/todayinenergy/detail.cfm?id=9871).

Wang, Amy B. "SRP Chief Will Lead Arizona Super Bowl Committee: Arizona Set to Host Super Bowl in 2015." AZcentral.com, March 26, 2012. Retrieved July 29, 2013 (http://www.azcentral.com/news/articles/2012/03/26/20120326srp-chief-lead-arizona-super-bowl-committee.html).

Whiteface Lake Placid. "Olympic Center." Retrieved
August 1, 2013 (http://www.whiteface.com/facilities/
olympic-center).

Wolfe, Michael. "Sport-Related College Degrees."
Synonym. Retrieved July 20, 2013 (http://classroom
.synonym.com/sport-related-college-degrees
-2512.html).

YMCA of Central Ohio. "Available Positions."
Retrieved July 20, 2013 (http://ymcacolumbus
.org/employment/available-positions).

INDEX

ABOUT THE AUTHORS

Kathy Furgang is a writer who has been writing educational books for teens for many years. She has written books about volunteer and internship programs in various professions. She also writes teacher guides and textbooks for students in elementary and middle school.

Adam Furgang is a professional writer who specializes in the middle school and high school educational market. His books include topics such as nutrition, the environment, health and disease, and science. He also writes fiction and has a background in fine art and graphic design.

PHOTO CREDITS